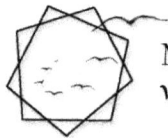

Mercury HeartLink
www.heartlink.com

Arranging
the
Constellations

Arranging
the
Constellations

ROBB THOMSON

Arranging the Constellations
Copyright ©2013 Robb Thomson

ISBN: 978-0-9892882-5-5
Publisher: Mercury HeartLink
Printed in the United States of America

Book design by Mercury HeartLink
www.heartlink.com, editor@heartlink.com

Cover portrait and interior portrait by Eric Thomson

Contents

DEBTS AND GIFTS

WHEN THE WORLD WAS NEW

WRESTLING WITH ANGELS

*for the El Castillo Writing Group and its leader,
Tanya Taylor Rubinstein, who have been
my chief writing mentors*

Intimations

THE NEST

An artful nest hangs from
A branch near the top
Of a tree. The bird,
Who builds only for itself is plain,
But the nest in its elegance
Completes the wholeness
Of tree and limb. Even the smallest detail—
Over which the bird toils—reflects
That entirety.

CLOSET SHELF

Hidden away on the top shelf
Of my bedroom closet, as a child,
I launched rocket ships to far planets,
Fought off space pirates
With my Buck Rogers blaster,
And saved Earth from Martians.
Sometimes, I just wondered who
I was growing up to become.

Now, in my dotage, I have another
Shelf, as I find myself lying in bed
Waking slowly, rearranging the constellations
Of my life, as if they were pictures in a room.
I sense Beauty at work here, and ask Her
How, like the Ancients who drew magic
From star-lit heavens, I might most artfully
Place the lights in my own skies.

So I stir up the tamped fire She first lit
Among the torn linens of my old shelf,
And feel her guiding hand,
As the embers fly.

INTIMATIONS OF JOY

The morning slowly gains its feet
Through a lifting fog of awareness
And a tangled sheet. Bits of dreams
Flit from my mind, leaving imprints
In the hardening mud of memory.

And from these ingredients, a day
Takes shape mixed with unfinished business
From a previous day, and imperatives
That stamp the landscape
Of all days.

But I hold a joker to give this day
A direction only I can see, and play
With this and that like a child facing
A candy dish, imagining tastes,
Before making the final choice.

As I lay each joker on the table,
I give tragedy a face of my own
And not tragedy's, and when the wind
Is right, I can sail round a headland
Into a beautiful day not known before.

But I forgot to mention that I do all this
While I hug you tight,
And the joker comes
Not from one hand,
But two.

My Garden

At my grandmother's knee, I learned
To count angels from Heaven's palace guard,
As they patrolled the border enclosing
The garden of my childhood.

That garden still fills my dreams,
And led me in adult days
To draw plans and employ professionals
To rebuild it. But I found none
Able to penetrate its inscrutable secrets.

Now in failure, I wonder—
Has my garden hidden itself
In the mystical entrails of my soul?
In last resort, I beg obliging genii
For guidance,

As I dissolve into the frailty
Of languorous song, fall recklessly
Into myself, and fracture all day's senses.
There, in sweet reverie, I discern
The Presence that hovered over my garden,

And, cradled in its arms, the child
Of old memory beckons to me.

THE BROKEN POT

Like the Native American breaks
Her pot when it has served its purpose,
The human is told to acquiesce
When his tiny contribution
To evolution's march is made.

But what of my pot's
Exquisite beauty—the best I can manage?
Must its living spirit be wasted
By an antiquated biology's
Rule of death?

Two Elderly Ladies

"I don't want to die on a Thursday,"
Said one lady friend,
As we sat at lunch with another.
I think secretly about such macabre things—
Never out loud in conversation.

But these two are different.
The entire lunch conversation veers
From funny tale about a funeral
Held for a person while still living,
To one about the dying patient

Who refuses last rites, because "God
Himself is looking after me."
One of them reminds me I better be ready
"Cause you don't want that last moment
To come as a big surprise."

What has she learned about that moment
That will change it for the better?
And even if it is better, why should I labor
Over a single moment with no future,
When all those others come before?

THE LAST OF THE TRIBE

It is only I for whom that Long Ago
Is still a living presence—

A small house peopled by a vibrant family,
Depression-damned parents,
And Depression-taught kids
Surviving at the edge.

The reality of that tiny microcosmic family,
And the frail tentacles
That bound us together
Has all but evaporated into silence.

But we remain in the grip
Of those now ghostly ties,
Like an ancient gnarled piñon tree
Rooted to the earth by

The once-living wood,
Covered by a patchy membrane of
Now-living bark,

The form of the whole lovingly composed
Of the one intertwined with the other.

PRAYER

At my grandmother's knee, when I said
"Now I lay me down to sleep ... "
Those angels were real and comforting.
But that business about dying
Didn't make much sense.

Now that I'm older, the person
I thought was there turns out to be
A mirage, something like Santa Claus.
If nobody's out there,
What can prayer be about?

Perhaps I look in the wrong place!
If there is no one
Out There,
There is certainly someone
In Here,

Where, unguarded, I can open myself,
And commune with what I find there.
That person is not quite the every day
Me I know, but something beyond, ineffable,
And much more me than me.

Patient, but often painfully critical,
Usually he speaks in the everyday here and now.
But sometimes his voice comes from somewhere
Beyond, from a timeless and limitless place,
Only vaguely sensed, but more real than real.

And in that other place, I feel your presence.
The you I know, and the Thou beyond you.
So that the love I share with myself and you
Mysteriously engulfs that larger field,
Where all life lives.

Now the prayer I knew as a child
Returns in a new glory and a new rapture,
The meaning which surrounded me then,
Grips me with all its earlier force.

LOVE SONGS

HER GRIN

As she stands on a rock at the pinnacle
Of Mount Baldy in my old photo, her hair
Blows in rivulets straight back in the wind,
And with only blue sky surrounding her,
The horizon far below, she welcomes
Me into her ecstatic privacy with a grin.

That youthful moment seems to have been
Blown far out to the edge of my memory
By the peak's eternal wind, where it shines
Like a lantern tied to the bow sprit
Of my life, now bound forever with hers
From that first invitation.

Our moment on the peak served us well,
Till, instead of old age beckoning us
To the quiet pride of richly lived lives,
Alzheimers stilled the wind.
In the ensuing quiet, the photo infects
Me with her timeless joy.

Honeymoon on a Bike

That morning, after a hurried wedding
By a handy seminary student,
They mounted their balloon tired single speeds,
With gear dangling from the frames at impossible angles,
And sailed North as two royal carriages
Breasting rush hour traffic.

Evening found them barely beyond the NW
Suburbs in farm country breathing irregularly
Through parched lips, and weaving wildly
On a straight smooth dirt road,
When they crashed in a heap of bicycles,
Tent, canteens, and wrapped sandwiches.

Flat on the ground, they looked through tears,
To see the dirty disheveled and bruised
Human beings they had become.

Gone were the impossible ideals,
Gone the glow of magic,
Gone the sexual desire.

In their place,
Two grinning pixies
Having fantastic fun.

LOVE SONG

You buried your head
In my chest
At the loss of our newborn.
Artless, like children,
We gave each to each
In plain wrapping.

IN THE KITCHEN

A saucepan in her hand,
She peers over her specs at me
With eyes that say "This is my kitchen,
But you can watch."
With the wink she throws at me
Between stirs, she tells me,
Though I don't belong,
I am very much part of the plan.
The grin on her face teases me
With the joke she is preparing
To spice her emergence from the kitchen.

The Asphodel

W. C. Williams wrote about
The Asphodel, a colorless odorless flower
That grows in Hell. About his search
For his wife's love, and how he found
Something, (if not that) on a field there.

We met on a mountain top,
But hurt and injury came
As we descended to lower regions,
Where we learned to hurt, and even to launch
Great harm in the service of Love.

Now shriveled by contradiction,
And lost in the un-silence of memory,
I roam the fields of that pale flower
Where, fragile as life itself,
Love does not conquer,

When a whisper comes back:

"In faith and loyalty,
I bring thee Home."

A Bequest

I stepped away from her now motionless bed,
And stumbled outside into the sun's day
And the mountain's blue.
With their geologic strength, they seemed
To take up the rhythm of her struggle
As Nature's own pulse, and passed it on to me.
As I breathed the breath, now bequeathed to me,
That she could no longer take,
It was sweet in my mouth,
As I shared its joy with her.

SHE

I find her presence
In unexpected joints
Of time and place
Here and there, now and then,

As unquiet memory
Shaves off slivers of joy
Mixed with spasms
Of guilt and anger.

But I cannot make her smile
When I try.

THE LEDGE

On the high rocky ledge
Where I flung her ashes
Into the peopled valley below,
I hear the murmurs of generations
In the play of the wind ...

Sounds of laughter, of lovemaking,
Babies crying, and the child who was
To be my great great grandmother
Playing jacks.

When I have become that wind,
What will people hear?

ODE TO NIGHT

Night is a thing of shadow, when
The shadows of day are released from objects
And become the objects themselves
In the reverse brightness of moon and stars.

The colors of shadow range from
The deep space black of a hopeless soul
To the infrared warmth of your love.
In the bendable time of the shadow world,
The feel of you becomes as real

As when your hair brushed my cheek,
And despair was banished by
The starlight shining in your face.

WITH AL

At ease in front of a partly reflecting
Window, a garden of humming birds
And butterflies beyond, we recalled
In silence our years of brotherhood.

Now, our two reflected faces overlapping
That garden vision continues to appear,
Wraith like, in my evening reveries.

At Lunch

The new resident sits demurely
Across from me, draped in an old
Red shawl. A brooch depicts
A hawk in flight, and her necklace
Catches my eye with its emerald.

Her suit, tasteful and quiet,
Leaves the jewelry to announce
Her singularity. She grew up,
She tells me, in my home town,
And when she mentions going

To my grammar school, I suddenly
Recognize her as the distant
Beauty in pigtails who always beat
Me in math at the blackboard.
Moving to another town, she went

Into the same field of research as I,
And lunch becomes a picnic
As the pigtailed girl, again before me,
Talks about working out puzzles
That always stumped me.

DEBTS AND GIFTS

MAMA

The Wilsons moved into a tumbledown house
Down the block. He was a terminal tubercular,
She a new mother, and the older kids
Neighborhood bullies, at whose hands
I bit the dust more than once.

When Mr. Wilson finally passed away
In terrible gasping pain,
The bullies went mute and passive,
While my mother became Grandma Thomson
To the big kids, and Mama to the baby girl,
As Mrs Wilson went to work.

We, her first kids,
Were certainly jealous,
But mainly just struck dumb,
Wondering
Where she got all that love from.

She said Christ had it,
And He said He got it direct from God.
So that is where I figured she got it—
Straight from God.
And no one said where God got it.

THE MODEL T

A great boxy mean-spirited thing,
With its innards right in your face,
My dad's second hand Model T
Was an essential part of my growing up.

It had to be hand cranked,
And when it ran, you could see its parts
As they jiggled and rolled,
In their splendid cacophony.

Model T's may not have had bailing wire
In their guts at first, but ours had twisted ends
Coming at you from all directions,
With more added at every fixing.

Indeed, I was the Apprentice
In charge of cutting the wire
To required lengths, and seeing
That the final twisted ends curled under.

One afternoon, the Ford was struck by lightning
While Dad was under it. After an anxious moment,
He emerged, wide eyed, to say
"The bolt fixed the problem."

When Dad later flipped it in a sharp turn,
I was delivered gently into his lap.
As Dad and the bystanders bounced
The "T" back on its wheels,

I realized my fondness for it was returned,
And never after was it equaled in my sight.

THE SWITCH

I discovered my big brother's
Treasure trove of Indian head pennies,
And sneaked them out a few at a time
To the candy store down the street.
The first trip was heady.
But then it got easy, and the candy was delicious.

Finally, my sweet tooth assuaged,
And the pennies gone,
The peace of the house was broken,
And Hell was being paid.
Without a pause, the finger pointed at me.
How the heck did they know?

My brother wanted to kill,
But instead I was instructed to
Cut a switch from the front yard tree,
And with slowly growing stiffness
And multiplying twigs,
Something suitable to my mother was produced.

Then in my shorts,
I got the full measure on my legs.
I thought skin covered those legs,
But not so—
They were naked nerve ends,
And I could only bawl and screech.

But as I hid in the closet, my tortured
Conscience morphed into the physical stings,
Which healed even as my bawling
Became a whimper,
And I emerged from the closet
Whole again in body and spirit.

THE CIRCUS

The circus came to town
And we all went to the parade.
But who was going to see the show?
Dad told us to pick the ripe tomatoes
From the back yard and sell them
From our red wagon.

So we started through the neighborhood,
And soon became a riotous Kid's
Parade when our young friends
Came running to join us. In spite
Of the depression times,
The tomatoes were soon gone,

And later that day,
From our front row seats,
The lions were deafening.

THE LOTTERY

My mother entered the lottery
When I was six years old,
Intending to win a new Austin mini-car,
To replace the Model T my Dad
Had in bits and pieces on the street.

This was Depression time,
And even necessities came hard,
So the lottery was played out
Around our fireplace like a fairy tale.

When we went down to see the Austin,
It purred like a cat as we patted it,
And we talked about how my mother
Would learn to drive, and we would glide
Through town as the new Thomson royalty.

Happiness and anticipation reigned
During the days leading up to the drawing;
We were untroubled by the odds,
Because fate had winked at us
To confirm the 'fix' arranged in our favor.

When the inevitable happened,
And the undeserving winners drove off in our car,
We could not believe such injustice
Could take place in open daylight.

MY OLDER BROTHER

I had never seen an opera before,
And Wozzek was a new world
Of sophistication and horror --
With its riveting story of humanity
Nailed to a modern cross.
My mother would never have allowed
Her son of fourteen to hear and see such.

But my battered brother knew
All the ways a mere human can fail.
So, as a fallen minister and rejected lover,
He set out to warn his younger brother,
And, in this city far from home,
He led me gently through my rite of passage.

He warned of the sickness unto death
That hazarded the adult world when courage
Failed, but like any nimble boy, I intended
To skirt those wastes with the laughter of youth,
And occasional help from the goddess of beauty
Who, according to him, smiled on all boys and men.

As I later walked the path
Laid out in those hours, and fell into
The human abyss first opened to my eyes
In that long ago opera, the guardian goddess
He first invoked for me wiped my brow
And lovingly pointed to the next leg.

WAR AT HOME

It had been waiting to happen,
When my brother and I ganged up
On Dad over Roosevelt's New Deal.

He knew in his gut it was deeply flawed,
But intuitions from his poor rural schooling
Were no match for our latest college educations,
And his defeat turned upside down
His deep pride in his sons.

He could never after share through me
My successes, and help with my failures,
And 'Dad' was relegated to a second order
Person I had to imagine,
And me to a single parent child.

And what of him?
The murder of his fatherhood
Denied him the right to live through
These sons, and he turned away
To something and someone else,

If he could find it.

MENTORING

The big difference between the kid
I mentor and me is I have played
This game just once, and wonder what
Would happen if I threw those dice again,
While he looks at me to find out
What kind of dice they are.

WHEN THE WORLD WAS NEW

PROLOGUE

How do I find words
to try the furthest limits of words,
find a music
to puncture thought,
and draw harmony from
the resonances of my heart
to free
the joy in my soul?

LIFE

If it were not so funny, it would be laughable;
If without love, hateful;
If without beauty,   pointless.

SHE WHO IS BEAUTY

My heart synchronizes with the beat
Of the "Queen of the Night," my eyes
See God's hand in Botticelli's "Spring,"
And my brain seizes as it takes in
An elegant equation—confirming
That in those moments she takes us
By the hand into the only Paradise there is.

Those ancient paintings in caves
Lovingly limned by wise forebears
Give me certainty She has from the beginning
Been at a few chosen fingertips
As they scratched new being out of silence.
She came to them not by command,
Or priestly ritual, or the science of things,
And certainly not by invoking the empty rules
Of bearded masters.

She came when She heard the skirling
Sound of their fingers as they pawed
Helplessly at the void, and with a god's
Grace, opened them to Her world
So miraculously right in all its parts.

Becoming

Out of what ancient pain was my first borning?
Was I brewed in the bowels of stars
To just the right consistency,
And then tempered in a cooling oven
To bring out the flavor?

Was I the skin of a paramecium
Before I parted company from
My mother and became me?
And are the bad times in those long eras
But gestation of new possibilities?

Even the ancient hills
Shout silently of their birth,
Of peace as a rare thing,
To be snatched a shred at a time,
Between eons of tragedy and turmoil.

Memory of the pain of all this mothering
Hints at a royal lineage and a god's strength
Flowing untapped in deep
Underground aquifers.

Backyard Tree

At four years, I used to
Climb up to the low crotch
Of an enormous backyard tree,
And sit there looking round
The yard as birds do.

I heard there that
The tree and the birds
Carried on deep conversation
About the vast world they saw,
And that only the bird's part
Of that conversation could be heard
By adult human ears.

But cuddled in the embrace
Of that ancient tree,
Its subsonic nursery song
Was as comforting as anything
My mother ever sang.

It told me how First Tree
Was cloned to make a forest,
And how trees once ruled the world,
Until God, without thinking,
Created a funny little two legged
Creature who could make axes.

The tree opened its world to me
As with light from a different

Part of the spectrum. It told how
The birds scouted for the trees
All the strange happenings
Visible from its top.

As I grew, the tree invited me
To crawl up a branch
To another juncture, and another,
Till the whole tree became
My play yard in the sky.

From one high horizontal branch,
I could look down into the grape arbor.
From another, I could step onto the roof
Of the house, and yet another led
Into a leafy hiding place
Where I could dream tree-dreams.

In later life, I returned to that back yard,
And the tree was gone.
I still wonder if perhaps I carry
In me a part of its spirit, which explains
Why I cringe when I see an old tree felled,
And erect bird houses round my house.

My Puff

After Listening to Peter, Paul and Mary

I'll never forget my Puff,
A magical dragon and creature
Of lyrical fire, who taught me the catch
Of joy, when laughter and music
Were top languages.

He wafted me through the stars
And around the moon.
As clocks went slowly backward,
In a physics not yet understood,
We sailed under a sea with man-fish
Of great wisdom.

When I got too big to ride him,
And forgot the finer points of flying,
I was captured by tentacled teachers
Sitting in classrooms, who apprenticed me
To Manhood.

But under their flatland stories lay
A land of Make-believe they seemed
Not to see. Though it seemed a matter
Of shame to them, it was easy to spot
My familiar landscape, from whose

Seditious music and myth all their
Loves and joys were forged.

WHEN THE WORLD WAS NEW

When the world was new,
And the stars were bright, all creation
Shimmered in my delight.
And God promised their secrets
Would be mine if I would but ask
The right questions.

But what to ask?—That childhood view
Of a sweeping tapestry was
Stitched into something even vaster,
And written in an abstruse mathematics
Unknown to my father and teachers.
In time, mentored by the masters,

I learned that script, caught glimpses
Of concealed structure, and pasted
My own human sized marginalia
On the sacred fabric. Now, in my dotage,
I clutch my treasure of secrets, as I once did
My stash of polished stones,

And laugh with God over our shared romp.

Poem and Poet

I sit down to write a poem,
Maybe about God, maybe about me.

In a rush, the words flow,
Line on stanza,
Like a Quixote charge,
Until the end,
When the summation
Makes no sense, and the joke is sprung.

What went wrong?
It was such a great idea.
But the first line led to the right,
And the Poet went left,
Losing meaning with
Awkward metaphor.

Without truth,
The poem is only a jingle
And Swinburne-like
Becomes a tickle
Instead of forked lightning,
Or even a pickle.

BROKEN TOWN

Piles of unfinished papers and open
Journals filled the study of the great
Scientist I'd come to see. It was a place
So far removed from my student world,
I sneaked a look for a wizard's
Hat he might keep under his desk.

But as soon as he settled me
In a comfortable chair, he drew me
Like a kindly father into his world,
And sent my mind flying with new ideas
That kept me working
At my farthest limits for years.

As I left his study, still in its spell,
While walking down their street,
Genial neighbors materialized
On their impeccable lawns
To assure me that anyone invited
To that house would be prized by all.

My spell was deepened by the canopy
Of greenery above the street, held against
The sky by trunks spaced like Grecian
Columns. It seemed in this town genius,
Community, and Nature had found
A timeless synthesis.

Years later, however, I returned to find
My aged mentor attacked by furious neighbors
For subverting the minds of their children.
They intended to replace his Godless science
In the school curriculum with Creationism.

Only dead stumps remained of the trees.

The Turn

A dirt road to the right of the highway
Beckons me into the mystery of myself.
As I turn into that road
I feel a hint of warning:

Will this turn into my uncertainty
Lead to a blank question,
Like the void that bounds
The infinity of possibility?

And will that continuum of roads
Into and beyond myself
Shrink me into a smallness
From such limitless choice?

And how do I know
Which choice may
Lead into a darkness
From which I cannot return?

Yet, I make the turn.

Appalachian Ghost

Muddy and exhausted, we were munching
Trail food, when a bearded apparition
Materialized out of the fog and rain,
And bounced into our midst, his cooking pan
Jangling from his old fashioned pack.

A jolly ancient Santa without a red coat,
He laughed and joked about how he
Was late getting to Mt. Katahdin,
Wished us a drier hike, and stomped
Up our back trail.

He may not have been real, but his
Effect was, as the puddled trail became
A linear string of pearls, and the mountain
Itself a veiled woman smiling at us
Through the mist with Eastern allure.

The rain sound had become the swish
Of a snare drum as Nature danced
Before us. We sat, soaking up the magic,
Before taking up our lightened packs
To steal on.

IN A HURRY

My life hurried on today,
Though I wanted to explore
The strange places along the way,
Their teases and tastes
Not to be found again.

So at evening, I dream about the day
And find understandings totally missed,
Beauties only glimpsed, and bring
Closure to a world that rushed,
And would not slow.

THE FUNK

Who knows the Funk?
That fellow who sucks the nerve from your body
In one big slurp, leaving you paralyzed
With all sphincters open.

I first encountered him
As a very ill child with
'Complications' to the flu,
The choked tears of my terrified mother
Dripping onto my fevered face.

In adolescence, with draft age approaching,
I saw sidelong each day's roaring news of war,
And would readily trade the coward's
Slap in the face for the shrapnel
In the gut or the charging bayonet.

Those early brushes with death
Made the Funk a frequent visitor
To the nights of my soul.
Till once, helpless in his grip
During an unprepared lecture,

A Me I never knew laughed aloud at him
With a mocking glee. Now, newly armed,
I and the funk are more evenly matched,
And when I merely wink,
He often slinks away.

Proverbs of the Old

When a teen, I delivered the newspaper
To the "Old Folks' Home." It had a musty
Smell about it, and its inhabitants a slow edgy gait,
As if they had to relearn how to walk
With each step. I was not sympathetic,

And looked on them as if at a world
Already in the history books. My future was
Tangible, already on my leash, and toward which
I was being pulled as by a big dog. My dog would
Have jerked those old ones off their feet.

Now I live in one of those "Homes,"
And realize the tentative walk results from
Pain, loss of balance and failing strength.
But I am not jealous of the young.
I eagerly taste my glowing days,

And the evening dusks they inevitably become.
I am still learning the fearlessness
That follows wisdom,
And the meekness to know that as a human
I can cause hurt when I love.

These essentials and the cool joy
They bring were far from my youthful
Understanding, and doled out sparingly
As door prizes along the way.
Now my aged step

Is a badge of honor I deeply prize,
And on my rheumatic knees,
I thank whatever gods there be
For the privilege of playing
At humanity awhile.

Wrestling with Angels

A GHOSTLY LAND

In the dusk along the foot of the Ghost cliffs
Many colors layer the ages back
To the oldest purple Chinles.
The rocks speak to me in whispers,
Radiating colors not seen in daylight.

It is a place of upside down strangeness,
As if a worm hole opened to greater
Depths of wisdom and consciousness
Astonishingly gentle with my kind.

Our conversation meanders in step
With the shallow breathing of the dusk,
Till I gasp, when the cliffs welcome me,
With their own paint brushes,
To make a new beauty to set alongside theirs,

If I can.

Goddess of the Commons

Song and story fill the air as I wander
The crooked village lanes at the core
Of my collective memory -- wonder stories
Of earth mother, of victory of good
Over evil, of God as Love become man.

But as I stray beyond those archaic precincts,
Discord mounts, and under the noon sun of science,
The mythic Goddess atop my village's gate
Is forced in retreat, to take her place
As wraith in memory's basement.

From there, she beckons me to the garden
At the heart of my village commons,
Where, entangled in the vines of old
And new fruit, we compose the melody
And myth that still structure my day,

And harmonize them to my village's
Ancient figured bass.

A Long Night

With the stink of death constricting
My breath, I stare, but cannot see the glow
That used to appear in the East.
I fear the sun has lost its daily battle
With night, and may be on its way to hell.

In night's solid grip, I set up a shrine
In my cell to all those remembered daybreaks,
Gestate new strength in the secret dark,
And plan subversive possibilities
For the new dawn.

Two Survivors

Wind from the centuries
Sighs from the depths
Of a Juniper tree, as it stands
Sentinel on the rim of a badlands.

A sliver of living bark
Winds its way around a desiccated
Branch, vestige of its youth,
To a scraggly outcrop of needles and berries
To confirm its treeness.

Feeling the wind in my human bones,
I stand on that bleak cliff,
And share its victory.

LAMENT FOR A RIVER

I know a River that isn't a river.

It used to be one before I knew it,
When it gurgled its joy, and could be fished.
Now, it is a River only because of the sign
Beside the big ditch it dug for itself,
And old stories about how it would flood
The town and my apartment in its exuberance.

If you sit still on its bank, you can barely
Hear a sobbing whisper, as the River
Laments its condition. Like an aged man,
It remembers when First People
Walked softly on its bank,

And its waters became the lifeblood
Of their communities.
It remembers when First Horse riders
Farmed its flood plain, and combed
Its long hair through the acéquias
Threading their villages.

But then came a final pulse of newcomers,
Grasping for every drop of water,
Who dammed up the River, so it gasps now
Only fitfully when they permit a trickle
Down the gully to water the cottonwoods
Along its banks, where forgetful birds nest.

ANTS

The ant works her head off
As part of an organism buried
In the earth, where I am told
Every caste labors in the service
Of the colony.

There must be ant-pleasure when
She finds a sweet smelling new pile
Of food and lays a back track, or
When feeding or being fed—
I guess that would be ant-love.

There must be ant-fear when she
Sees a nest predator, ant-buddying
As she teams up to repel the enemy,
And ant-celebration when the
Enemy is defeated.

But I see no personal ambition
In any ant. Their colony is the One God,
And there are no tempting trees
Of Knowledge or Life in their Eden.
Pity the ants.

THE BRUTES

Night and day, my genes fight it out
In the lidded pit where I keep my biology.
Some follow the Dawkins-Law of constant conflict.
Others the Village-Law of loyalty
And tribe-wide altruism.

There is constant howling and screaming
For my attention from that infernal pit,
And I lean to pet those that know
How to fashion feelings of endearment
For members of my tribe.

But in dreams I realize the farthest leap
My soul can make from me to thee
Defines the outer boundary of my tribe—
Beyond which I hear only shouts
Of hate from even the most cuddly
Of those pit brutes.

So where do I find a humanity
I can stretch endlessly to kiss
Those misty faces in far places?
And how do I entangle my pit relatives
With the gossamer nothings I
Contrive in dreams?

REMEMBERING THE RAIN

It was so parched
That when the rain began,
Even the concrete of the street took a long
Drink before rivulets could form.

It was the beginning of the Great Dry,
When we learned our beloved
West, which had already lost much
Of its forests to fire and insects,
Was to be no more.

Like the old villages
Once strung across a green Sahara,
We were to enter a period of desertification,
When water would become more precious
Than gold, and we'd learn to live
In an oxygen fed moon-scape,
Hostile as that of any foreign planet.

We will live in air conditioned cocoons
And pull the levers and push
The buttons that operate
The technologies designed to shelter us
From the hellish oven we are about
To make of the earth—

That once paradise
Which washed our nakedness
In gardens where the gods
Of our myths lived,
But will live no more.

The Cape of Lost Possibility

Sometimes I find myself in the mist
At the Cape of Lost Possibility,
In search for some central meaning
I fear has been missed,
Some beauty marred,
Some warning not heeded.

I have looked for a path back,
So we can try it all over again.
But our footsteps have disappeared,
And the way back is
Just another way forward, with all the
Mystery of any future.

It is an enormous egotism
That brings me here,
As if I can be guide to my whole tribe,
When I am only an atom in that organism.

But coming here is a necessary journey of grief,
To light a prayer candle of contrition
For a stumbling kin careening between
The poles of love and aggression,
Burping up saints and sinners in random confusion,
Making a cosmic racket like an unbalanced centrifuge.

What purpose does my mourning serve?
Do my tears bleed back

Like the slow drip of an intravenous feed
Into the body of a rampant populace
That knows no mirth?

I simply don't know,
But must moan
For my suffering tribe,
And broken earth.

December 7, 1941

I was seventeen,
And driving home from Church,
When the radio announcer broke
Into my peace to announce
The Japs had bombed Pearl Harbor.

In school next day, I sat
With the other seniors in Assembly,
As President Roosevelt called for war
And seemed to touch each of us on the shoulder
With an invocation of tribal loyalty and unity.

In those days, fear tore my gut, while threats
To my personal and collective being were enacted,
As by a continuous tape, on the screen
Of my mind -- the struggle on Guadalcanal
Supplying the graphics.

The term, "Japs," became our symbol
For pure evil, as we spat it through
Pursed lips, and I vowed my personal
Revenge for the gentlest boy
In my neighborhood and his stilled cello.

Four years later, I found myself
In the occupying force
On the landing that faced
What had been their greatest city,
But was now a charred desert.

Overnight, the Jap monsters of my
Four year nightmare disappeared,
As I entered a bombed out store,
To study the subtle woodblock prints
Of a starving artist of great mastery.

Some have said our tribe's finest hour
Was the war we fought against tyranny.
I think it was the hour when we stood
On their boat docks and in their art shops,
And embraced our suffering enemies.

TRUTH IN THE WILD

In my youth, I was caught in the daytime nightmare
Of world war driven by mob madness,
And my rational mind was a pimp in its service.
In the quiet that followed, with a sudden clarity,
I saw the suffering in the cities I had helped destroy,
And a stubborn people
Reviving from the ashes.

Even on less turbulent days,
Another self seems to float
Over the understory of my mind,
Isolated from its real motives,
As, piloting an airplane over a jungle,
I would be hidden from the animals
On the jungle floor. And I am as unable
To guide those biologically rooted forces
Roaming my jungle floor as to guide the hunt
Of any wild animal.

When my jungle sleeps, I am humbled
By how my inhumanity dominates
My being, and sense the eons of time since
Humans began to create a mistake-strewn path,
Making one choice after another toward
That little humanity we have achieved,

And sigh at the patience and forgiveness required,
As my jungle shadow wakens,
And we stumble back
Into the day.

ABOUT THE AUTHOR

Robb Thomson grew up in El Paso, Texas during the mid 20's to early 40's of the last century. He was educated at the University of Chicago and at Syracuse University, where he received a PhD in Physics. He spent a career in research and teaching on the faculties of the University of Illinois (Urbana) and The State University of New York (Stony Brook) and at the National Institute of Standards and Technology.

Thomson lives in Santa Fe, NM, and writes poetry because, as the most powerful language we have, it is a joyful guide to one's unfamiliar self, and an equally enlightening guide to the outside world we only thought we knew.

.

www.ingramcontent.com/pod-product-compliance
Lightning Source LLC
LaVergne TN
LVHW091314080426
835510LV00007B/491